PLEASE UNDERSTAND ME,
I AM YOUR CHILD

Please Understand Me, I Am Your Child

A book about attention
hyperactive disorder

GIVING PARENTS AN EDGE
ADHD: WHAT TO DO

Henry Mainville

To order additional copies of this book, contact:
Xlibris Corporation
1-888-795-4274
www.Xlibris.com
Orders@Xlibris.com

56483

CONTENTS

Introduction

The purpose of this book is to help parents understand their child with ADHD. Children with ADHD have difficulty functioning in three main areas: learning, social, and behavior. Also, we will talk about the pain of loss and grief parents who have children with ADHD often experience. Mostly we will discuss the best ways parents can help their children with ADHD. It is important to note that there are three different types of ADHD. ADHD describes the child who has difficulty functioning at home and in school because of hyperactivity and lack of impulse control. The second type is ADD, which describes the child who is not hyperactive but has a short attention span, lacks focus, and is easily distracted. The third and last type of ADHD is the combined type, which is when a child has all the symptoms we have just described. For the purpose of this book, we are mostly discussing the child with ADHD combined type.

ACKNOWLEDGMENTS

I would like to thank my wife, Roslyn, for her support and encouragement during the process of writing this book. Also, I would like to thank all of the teachers I have worked with over the years for all that they have taught me about children. I especially thank Karen Breault for suggesting the title of this book. Mostly, I want to thank the children and families who have helped me understand the challenges they face at home and in school.

Chapter I

Secrets from the Frontline

Then and now: What we have learned over time on how to understand and treat children with ADHD.

1. Even kids who are quiet and withdrawn can have ADHD.

2. ADHD is not diagnosed too much. It is not diagnosed enough.

3. Kids with ADHD are not stupid.

4. Kids with ADHD can learn to behave. They are not misbehaving to get attention.

5. Kids with ADHD can learn to get along with other kids.

When I was a student in elementary school many years ago, discipline was the norm. I attended a Catholic elementary school in Holyoke, Massachusetts, at that time the paper capital of the world. Classes were large with twenty-five to thirty-five students to a class, sometimes even more. The school went from kindergarten to eight grades. The nuns were our teachers, and they were very strict. I was afraid to interrupt them, even when I had to go to the bathroom. Most of us did not dare move while they were teaching. Some of us, despite our best efforts, were not able to sit still, be quiet and not interrupt. These children were sometimes sent to the principal's office. More often, the admonition of the teacher was enough for this child to get back on task. If a reminder did not work, the nuns would threaten to call the child's parents. Nobody wanted the sisters to call their parents. This threat caused great fear among the children since they knew that a phone call from sister meant corporal punishment at home. The parents always backed up the sisters when it came to discipline. The nun's authority was special and undisputed. Teachers, today, do not enjoy the same level of authority or respect. Parents and teachers were a team united to help their children behave and get along with people. Of course, physical punishment was not right or acceptable, but the unity of school and home was solid. This connection between school and home made it easier for children to learn proper behavior. As children grew older, especially in sixth, seventh, and eight grades, the teachers would sometimes use corporal punishment. I remember one incident in eight grades when a student was not following sister's directions and was being disruptive. She called him to the front of the class, brought him into a closet, and slapped his face so hard that he returned with a black eye. Many other students who misbehaved were smacked on the hand with a ruler. Sometimes, they were hit so hard the ruler broke.

Times have changed now, in many ways for the better. In other ways, the changes have not been beneficial. The lack of discipline in some schools does not create a good learning environment for students. Often, school and home are not united in establishing consequences for bad behavior. This creates a split between parents and teachers that does not help anybody, especially the students. Students who misbehave do not learn to make good choices. Students who are in the middle of the madness and trying their best also suffer. Although the nuns were excessively strict and sometimes abusive, the classroom environment was predictable and a good environment for learning. Now, however, after years of experience, I realize that those children who misbehaved in class were probably suffering from ADHD. Unfortunately, we did not know about ADHD when I was a child. If we had known, many children would have been spared much hardship and humiliation.

Many years later, when I began to see children and adolescents in therapy, we often did not know what prevented them from learning. As a result, we often did not understand the significance of loss and change in their lives. We hardly ever diagnosed children as depressed, bipolar, schizophrenic, autistic, or any other psychiatric diagnosis. Many parents and professionals then and even now do not understand how a child's mental health affects his performance in school, his relationship with peers, and his behavior. We professionals also did not understand why a child was not learning. To explain things, we would say that a child had minimal brain dysfunction or that he was limited. If a child did not behave, we would say that he was stubborn or obstinate. If a child could not get along with people, he was a loner. We did not label children as ADHD, conduct disorder, or oppositional defiant disorder. Each child was good or bad, smart or limited, social or isolated.

Over time, social workers, teachers, and psychologists have gotten better at understanding and helping children. Kids who cannot learn are seen as learning disabled. Children who do not have impulse control are diagnosed as ADHD. There are many other diagnoses that help us understand children such as speech impairment, depression, and bipolar. As a result of this progression in knowledge, we are now better able to understand children who have difficulty functioning in school, whether it is their ability to learn, to behave, or to get along with others.

We have learned to accept children as individuals with their own strengths and weaknesses. When I first started counseling children, I would always start by playing checkers or some other game in order to develop a relationship. I did not understand as I do now that children are individuals like you and me. They have the same struggles, the same hurts, the same pain, and the same feelings. Emotionally, children hurt as much, if not more than us adults. We have the benefit of experience. Children often do not have the capacity or knowledge that they can overcome hurt and pain like you and me. We need to teach them that hurt is temporary and that we can grow emotionally and socially. The difference between children and adults is that we have had many hurts and equally as many opportunities to learn how to cope. Children do not have that experience or knowledge of how to handle their emotional pain and hurt. We need to help them learn how to cope with these feelings. We have developed our own ways to deal with anger, with sadness, with rejection, with loss, and with all the other situations that cause us pain. Many of us have found spouses, friends, ministers, family members, and many other people to turn to when we need help. We also have learned what provides us comfort and gives us strength. For some, it is quiet and solitude. For others, it is seeking advice. For others, reading, sports, the arts, prayer, poetry, or many other activities can provide comfort.

Over time, I have learned to listen to children and to respect them. The main difference between children and us is that they go to school and we work.

What is important in both of these situations is that we are able to function to the maximum of our abilities. When a child or an adult stops functioning or has difficulty functioning, we need to look at the causes of this inability to succeed. We need to understand and help children get back on track. For adults, alcohol abuse, drug addiction, mental illness and physical disability are some of the reasons they stop functioning. For children, physical, mental, and emotional impairments inhibit their functioning. Unfortunately, there still are many parents and professionals who do not understand children. For example, parents and teachers still say things like this child is not behaving because he is seeking attention. We do not say that adults are seeking attention when they behave badly. We hold adults accountable for their mistakes. We also need to hold children accountable when they make bad choices. Of course, we are not going to arrest a child for getting into a fight. We do need to teach children right from wrong. More often than not, a child will get into a fight with another child because they lack impulse control. Also, children with ADHD will often disrupt a class by talking or walking around when they are bored because they have difficulty sitting still and listening to the teacher. Many parents do not see these problems at home. This is because children at home can play, watch TV, play computer games, run, have fun, and do things that they like. Very often, the only problems children have at home is following directions, getting along with their siblings, and doing homework. We need to help these children control their impulses and make better choices at home, but especially in school.

CHAPTER II

THE EXPERIENCE OF ADHD

ADHD *Is Not Fun*

1. Living in the moment has consequences.

2. ADHD kids get in trouble a lot in school.

3. Friends are hard to keep.

4. Being organized is not easy, maybe even impossible.

5. Giving up and not caring sometimes seems like the only answer for a child with ADHD.

In over thirty years of social work practice, I have seen hundreds of adults and children with ADHD. All of my clients, adults and children, share many similar characteristics. More than most of us, they all live in the present. This means that there is no before or after. People who do not have ADHD remember past events and are able to draw on those experiences to make present decisions. People who do not have ADHD can think of consequences when making a decision. They know that the present decision that they make will affect the after. Children and adults with ADHD very often cannot draw on past experiences to make future decisions.

The majority of ADHD people have difficulty with organization. Those with mostly attention issues are often distractible and have difficulty focusing on a task if it does not interest them. Interestingly, people with ADHD often hyper focus when watching TV or playing video games. They need to be called many times before parents can get their attention. In school, these problems with attention adversely affect a child's ability to learn. The inability to attend and the high level of distractibility means that ADHD children often miss much of what the teacher is trying to help them learn.

Those with mostly impulsiveness and hyperactivity are very restless and cannot sit still. They are often in trouble with other people because they act before they think. Also, they often make poor decisions because they do not think before they act. Behaving properly is a constant challenge for these children.

Because ADHD children are often active or inattentive or restless or impulsive, they do not learn the fundamental principles of social interaction. They do not listen to what other people are telling them. There is no give-and-take. ADHD children can be entertaining and draw other children to them by their energy and creative play, but they do not know when somebody might be upset with them. Also, they often do not know when their actions are inappropriate. As an example, they may be talking in class and not be aware that it is inappropriate to do this.

Emotionally, ADHD children have the same feelings as other children. Their problem is that they do not know how to regulate these feelings. For example, an ADHD child who becomes angry might just hit another child rather than talk about what made him angry. ADHD children are able to make friends, but the friendships often do not last. That's because the ADHD child has friends for the moment. He usually will go with the child that is fun and exciting. His relationships are immediate. He does not have the capacity to deeply understand the qualities his friend may have and to do all that is needed to sustain a friendship.

When asking parents about their ADHD child, parents will often respond, "I was like that when I was a kid." Heredity is a strong factor in ADHD. There is a strong correlation between children with ADHD and their parents. Very often, one parent had ADHD as a child even though it was not diagnosed when that parent was still a child. Estimates are that 70 to 80 percent of children diagnosed with ADHD have at least one parent with this issue. Parents will say things like "I had a behavior problem as a child or I could not pay attention or I was always distracted." Also, about 29 percent of siblings of children with ADHD will also have this condition.

Many adults and children describe their experience of ADHD in very dramatic ways. One woman says that as a child, she felt like bugs were crawling over her body, and therefore, she could not keep still. Another person, a sixteen-year-old teenager, said that she counted the tiles on the ceiling as her teacher was giving a lecture. An eleven-year-old child I was seeing described her experience in the classroom as being in jail while watching a crime scene. She was saying that she could not absorb or react to anything that was happening in the classroom because she was consumed with her own distracting thoughts and impulses. Other parents describe school as a traumatic experience because they could never succeed academically and were always in trouble. One parent recently told me that he spent most of his high school years in the mall rather than attending school. Many of these parents were never diagnosed as having ADHD. Our understanding of ADHD is a recent phenomenon. We now know that there is a direct link between ADHD and our brain. The ADHD child's brain works as if it has constant interference like a TV with bad reception or a computer that does not input the right information. In ADHD children, there is a very limited chance that the ADHD child will hear the instructions the first or even the second and third times they are given to them. Sometimes parents or the teacher can repeat the same directions a hundred times, and the ADHD child will still not remember what was said. It is because their inability to attend is so great that they do not register the direction in their brain. For some people, the old expression "In one ear and out the other" is true. If you don't hear, you cannot make the instruction part of you.

Children from ages three to twelve and later develop a program for living. They learn what is right from wrong, what to do when angry, what to do when they need something, how to get along, and how to solve problems. All of these situations require learning rules of behavior with regard to one's own personal behavior and in relation to other people. ADHD people have difficulty following steps and incorporating rules. ADHD people often go from problem to solution without much thought. The solution is often not the best. Most ADHD children will hit back if another child hits them. They react immediately and with no thought of the consequences. The ADHD child could get into trouble a thousand times for the same situation and still not think of a different and better solution. A more appropriate solution, of course, would be to tell the teacher. Of course, this solution would require stopping, thinking, and choosing not to react. The ADHD child does not think; he acts.

People often misinterpret the actions of ADHD children, especially negative behavior. People will say that the ADHD child who threw his book on the floor was doing it to gain attention. This is not true. ADHD children act on impulse most of the time. They do not say to themselves, *I am going to throw this book on the floor to get attention.* They just throw the book without thinking. ADHD children act impulsively. That means they act without planning ahead or thinking of the consequences. Because most people think that ADHD children behave badly deliberately, they are often critical and negative toward the ADHD child. As a result, the ADHD child often sees himself as bad and has low self-esteem. The low self-esteem extends to almost everything in his life, including school, friends, home, and especially his sense of self. Very often, the ADHD child loses hope and begins to not care about anything.

Chapter III

ADHD: What to Do About Learning

DONT SHOOT THE MESSENGER

1. Don't blame the teacher when she says that your child is not learning.

2. Learning disabilities and ADHD are two different diagnoses.

3. Your ADHD child is going to need a lot of help from you to do his homework.

4. If the social worker or teacher says that your child might have ADHD, it is important you seek medical help.

5. If your child is not learning, he is not stupid or lazy. He might have ADHD.

The ADHD child is at a huge disadvantage in school. Unlike home, school is a very structured environment where much is expected of the child. Focusing, paying attention, organizing, remembering, listening, following directions, and sitting still are essential skills that every child needs to learn. The ADHD child, depending on the severity, does not have some or all of these skills. Without these skills, the ADHD child misses huge amounts of learning that he needs to succeed in school. Schools are built on the premise that learning takes place in stages. For example, to learn to read, a child first needs to know the alphabet. He also needs to be able to decode the words he reads. Once the child has these skills, he can begin to understand what he reads. The same gradual accumulation of knowledge applies to developing math, writing, and other concepts. The ADHD child often misses out on the basics and, therefore, cannot proceed to the next stages of learning. While other children progress, the ADHD child is left behind and cannot keep up academically with the rest of the children. As the years progress, the learning gap between the ADHD child and other children grows. This has disastrous consequences for the ADHD child. Not only does the ADHD child fall behind academically, he also often begins to have social and behavioral difficulties. The ADHD child's self-esteem begins to suffer. Before long, not having much if any academic success, the ADHD child begins to not care about school and learning. Years of instruction are wasted. The ADHD child gives up on school and learning. What a tragedy for the child and for society. The child does not reach his potential, and society does not get the benefit of that child's later contribution to society. In fact, ADHD children who are never treated for this condition often end up using drugs or alcohol as adults. Studies show that there is a strong correlation between ADHD and SUD, which is short for substance use disorder. Adults with ADHD are twice as likely to have SUD compared with those who don't have ADHD. Up to 25 percent of adult drug addicts and alcoholics currently have ADHD. Also a high percentage of people in prison have ADHD that never was treated. Among adolescents, up to forty-six percent who are in the juvenile justice system have ADHD.

There is hope for children with ADHD. One time, after years of my trying to have some parents consult with a child psychiatrist regarding their child's ADHD, they agreed and put their child on medication. The results were dramatic. This child was in fifth grade at the time and about two years behind academically. Within a week of being on medication, this child exclaimed happily, "I'm smart. I can learn." Within a year, the child had caught up academically and graduated fifth grade on the same academic level as his peers. Needless to say, the parents were delighted and relieved that their child could learn, and so was the child. There are other children, depending on the severity of their ADHD and on their inherent natural ability, that get by in school and get passing grades from one year to the next. These children, however, never reach their potential. Again, this is a huge loss to them and to society.

The school environment is structured, focused, and demanding. This is necessary in order for children to learn and for teachers to be able to teach. Students and teachers would not be able to function in a disorganized and chaotic environment. Like a lot of situations, a structured school environment works for most children, but not so well for ADHD children. Why is this? As mentioned above, the ADHD child is not focused, structured, and organized. School is like work. If a carpenter wants to build a house, he needs the right tools. For a student to learn, he also needs the right tools. Two of these tools are focusing and paying attention. Others are organization, listening, following directions, and memory. Being able to sit still is also very important. For now, let's talk about focusing and paying attention. The modern classroom is fast paced.

A lot of learning takes place in a short amount of time. Also, the curriculum is designed like building blocks. The student needs to master the first-grade curriculum in order to understand and learn what is taught in second grade. Each grade builds on the other. That is why focusing and paying attention is so important. The ADHD child is at a huge disadvantage. When a child is not paying attention or not focused on what is being taught, he often misses crucial information in every class that he attends. This means that in the following class, that child may not be able to follow what is being taught because of information that was missed in a previous class. Worse, missed information has a cumulative effect and makes it harder and harder as that child advances from grade to grade. It is like the builder who misses important parts of the foundation and, therefore, cannot safely start building the first floor.

An ADHD child could benefit greatly from a small classroom with a trained special education teacher. This type of class reduces distractions, provides more structure than a regular education class, helps the child focus, and allows the teacher to give individualized instruction. Unfortunately, these classes are rare in public schools at this time because of changes in federal and state guidelines for special education. The new trend in public education is for inclusion in the regular classroom regardless of the student's disability. Still, when available, individualized or small group instruction with a resource teacher could benefit the ADHD child. Also, proximity to the teacher is helpful. The ADHD child needs much repetition of what is being taught. The ADHD child should often be asked to restate what he has learned. He may need additional cues when the teacher is giving directions. Visual cues are always helpful. A written step by step plan taped to the child's desk that the teacher could point to can be helpful. The plan could include a visual schedule of the day's activities as well as steps to take when writing or taking tests.

When reading, the ADHD child could benefit from reading challenging material three times: Once for basic meaning, a second time to read more carefully for details, and a third time to reinforce and promote long-term retention.

In addition to having difficulty learning in school, the ADHD child also has problems doing homework by himself. Doing homework requires a child to pay sustained attention and focus in order to complete the homework in a timely manner. Homework is not fun, it is work. In fact, it is hard work. The ADHD child is at a big disadvantage because the focus and attention homework requires are not skills the ADHD child has. The ADHD child can sustain attention like many of us when something is fun or entertaining like video games, TV, or a good book. Very often, I advise parents to reduce the distractions like noise when their child is doing homework. I also often suggest that they sit with their child when they are doing homework to redirect him when he loses focus. Homework is often hard but necessary work for the parents if they want their child to succeed. The same strategy is also used in class by teachers. Teachers will often have the ADHD child sit next to them while they are teaching. Often, when a child comes to my office for counseling, he will be looking out the window rather than at me. Anybody walking by or talking will distract the child from our conversation. Even with a quiet setting and playing a game that the ADHD child likes, it is very difficult for that child to pay attention to the task at hand. Another strategy to make homework easier at home is for the ADHD child to have only one subject on his desk at a time. This strategy is also helpful in the classroom. Also at home and in school, the teacher could use a timer that goes off every five minutes to remind the student to focus.

Another obstacle to learning for the ADHD child is organization. Teachers will often find that Sarah is very bright, but that she always forgets her homework. More often than not, this is an issue of not remembering and of not being organized. The ADHD child remembered to do his homework but did not put it in his backpack when he finished. To be organized, one has to remember all the steps needed to complete a task. If Mom says, "Go upstairs, brush your teeth, put on your pajamas, and shut off the lights," it is likely that the ADHD child may remember one or two directions and forget the third. I often suggest to teachers and parents to use one-step directions.

Also, a good strategy is to have the child repeat the direction after you have said it. This increases the chances that the child will in fact do what he is told. Doing papers or projects is especially hard for ADHD children because these tasks require long-term planning, timelines, and organization. Parents and teachers can help greatly with projects by breaking down the tasks required and setting timelines for each part of the project. Also, color-coded folders can be helpful. For example, you could have a red folder for math, a yellow folder for writing, and a green folder for social studies.

Listening and following directions are also hard for ADHD children. Generally, ADHD children have good hearing. The problem is that they can't stay focused long enough to hear what the parent or teacher is saying to them. They don't remember what to do because they never heard the directions. They were thinking about, looking at, or distracted by something else. Having the ADHD child repeat or write down the directions can be helpful. Sometimes, teachers and parents will say things like "He chooses not to listen to me," or "He does not want to listen to me." Other things people say are things like "He has an attitude," "He's not smart," and "He deliberately is defying me." All of these conclusions are wrong. How can an ADHD child, who acts on impulse 90 percent of the time, think and plan to be oppositional? Disobeying suggests that the child who is not following the rules has a rational ulterior motive to not listen. This cannot be true. Remember, we said that most often, the ADHD child acts on impulse. Impulse means acting without thinking. For the ADD child who is disorganized, distracted, inattentive, lacking focus and organization, deliberately planning to not listen seems far-fetched. Listening, following directions, and thinking before acting are all skills that the ADHD child does not have.

Another problem the ADHD child faces is restlessness. ADHD children, especially those with impulse control, have trouble sitting still. When the teacher is giving a lesson, she cannot have the children running around the room. This would be distracting to her and the children in the classroom. The ADHD child has a very limited capacity to sit still. It then becomes hard for him to pay attention long enough to learn what is being taught. Moving around is a distraction in itself and therefore interferes with learning. One strategy to use is a Move and Sit cushion. This cushion has nodules on it that seem to provide sensory stimulation that is calming to the ADHD child and helps with sitting still. It should be noted that the helpfulness of the Move and Sit cushion generally lasts only a few weeks to a month. Once the novelty of it has diminished, the positive effect of the cushion also ends. Also, tying a rubber band on the legs of the chair sometimes helps. The child can move his feet up and down on the rubber band rather than getting out of his seat. Over time, I have also noticed that ADHD children have a poor sense of space. For example, when walking along the hallway, they often need to touch the wall with their hand. They also often sit on their legs and move around a lot.

Sometimes they even fall off their chair. To remedy this, I have been telling children to anchor themselves in class. This means that they must sit on their behinds, put their hands on the desk and put their feet on the floor. Teachers have also been using this method and have found it to be helpful. Anchoring could be part of the visual schedule ADHD children tape to their desks.

Many strategies and ideas to help the ADHD child learn have been presented in this chapter. Teachers have many other strategies to help the ADHD child learn. The strategies presented in this book are those that, through much experience, seem to be the most helpful.

CHAPTER IV

WHAT TO DO ABOUT SOCIAL AND EMOTIONAL DEVELOMENT

Going along and getting along

1. Help your child accept responsibility when he gets into a fight.

2. Give your child strategies to deal with bullies other than hitting them.

3. Encourage your child to express his feelings.

4. Help your child deal with emotional pain by talking.

5. Forgiveness is often the best answer.

In recent years, many schools have begun to emphasize the social-emotional development of children. There seems to be a growing recognition that schools are not just about academic learning but also about social and emotional learning. Many schools have group meetings with kids where they learn about feelings and how to get along with others. These initiatives are usually developed by school social workers and psychologists. Sometimes, social skills and emotional literacy are also taught in the classroom by teachers and other professionals.

The development of social-emotional skills varies from child to child. Some children are very adept at making friends and expressing their feelings. Others are very limited in these skills, especially ADHD children. Other influences involved in social-emotional development are parents, siblings, extended family, neighbors, teachers, coaches, and other people children see every day. Also, some children are shy. ADHD children are usually outgoing. Shy children tend to stay by themselves. Outgoing children usually have a lot of friends. ADHD children often have a lot of friends but have problems sustaining friendships for a long time. This is because ADHD children often lag behind other children in their social-emotional development. Lack of impulse control and lack of empathy are two of the main reasons why ADHD children have difficulty with closeness, intimacy, and making lasting friends. They may seem to have a lot of friends, but these contacts are mostly superficial and without depth. Recently, a friend of mine whose mother died was surprised that his nephew who attended the funeral did not have any friends with him to provide support. My friend always thought that his nephew had many friends. My friend realized that his nephew had friends but that they were superficial. ADHD children do not have lasting or deep relationships. This is because they live mostly in the present. They lack empathy, they have difficulty regulating emotion, and they do not internalize social rules.

As we have discussed, ADHD children live mostly in the present. They seek action, not closeness. They want fun now, not tomorrow. They do not remember from day to day and therefore cannot build a bank of memories relating to the people they like. For most of us, friendship grows over time. As we become closer, the more shared experiences we have. The ADHD child lives mostly in the moment and does not have a bank of memories to fall back on when he is thinking about or missing his friend. The ADHD child does have friends. He often is the life of the party. Other kids like him because he is fun to be with. Children like action. They are often stimulated by the ADHD child. ADHD children have enormous energy. They do not stop doing, acting, running, and playing. They often say and do things that make other children laugh.

Another main factor in developing friendships is the ability to empathize with others. ADHD children lack empathy. They live from moment to moment. Empathy is the capacity to understand and relate to other people's pain and hurt. ADHD children often do not know when they have hurt another person's feelings. As they live in the present, it is hard, if not impossible, to reflect on what they did five minutes ago that might have been hurtful to another person. They have already moved on to the next fun activity. When the parent, teacher, or adult points out that you just hurt your brother or friend, they often truly are surprised. They do not know what you are saying until you explain it. This is because they cannot reflect easily on their past actions. Often, they themselves do not even know when another child has hurt them emotionally. To feel hurt, you need to be able to reflect on your own hurt as well as on what you did to hurt others. You also need to own and internalize those actions and words, that are wrong and hurtful to other people. Saying sorry and apologizing are very difficult for the ADHD child. Because they live in the moment and have not internalized good social behavior, they do not know when they have been hurtful to another person. You most often need to explain to the ADHD child what he did wrong. You need to go back in the past for him. You need to have the person that was hurt explain to the ADHD child what he did that was wrong. If ADHD children cannot empathize with others and even know when they have been hurt emotionally, how do they start and have relationships with other children? As we already have mentioned, this is because ADHD kids are fun to be with. Also mutual empathy in children is not as important as it is in adult relationships. Adults know, or at least should know, the unspoken rules of friendships and relationships. These rules include the capacity to empathize with the other person, to share and enjoy satisfying experiences with the other person, to tolerate and endure the inevitable ups and downs of relationships. They are all part of having close and lasting friendships and relationships.

Earlier, I had mentioned many initiatives schools have begun to develop social-emotional intelligence. Some of these ideas include social skills training in the classroom and groups outside of the classrooms where children can interact with each other and develop social skills. In my experience, however, the best way for children to develop the skills necessary to get along with people and to handle their feelings is a program introduced in our school in Stamford about ten years ago called Responsive Classroom. This is a program developed by social workers in Massachusetts that has been introduced in many schools throughout the country. In this system, the entire school follows a preset model of social, emotional, and behavioral expectations, which is like an added curriculum. The principal, the teachers, the students, and the professionals, and all other staff follow the same rules of behavior and social interaction. All of the staff is trained. A clear set of expectations is developed to help the children know what to do socially, emotionally, and behaviorally.

The school day is begun with a morning meeting where each child is given the opportunity to lead the discussion on a rotating basis. Three children are picked to share something about them. Often, it is a favorite toy or stuffed animal. It also could be a trip, an experience, or something else in their life. The other children are then invited to comment or ask a question. The meeting ends with the teacher telling the children what the schedule will be for the day. Sometimes the children are asked to read the schedule out loud. This meeting serves many purposes. It helps the children get to know each other. It also helps each child begin to feel comfortable talking about himself. Children also learn how to listen and take turns. Mostly, the morning meeting develops a unity and closeness in the classroom that sets a calm and trusting tone for the rest of the day. The social and behavioral rules of the classroom are explained at the beginning of the year and followed each day. If a child interrupts the classroom, criticizes another child, or does any other unwanted behaviors, he is given a warning by the teacher. If he continues his behavior, he is asked to go to the time-out chair and return to the class when he is ready to behave. If that does not help, he is asked to go to the buddy teacher where he stays until he is ready to return to class. As a last resort, an administrator is called. Also, children are asked to walk quietly in the hallways so as not to disturb the other classes. In this program, there are clear procedures to follow if a child insults, abuses, threatens, hits, steals, or does anything physically or emotionally to hurt another child. If a child is caught doing any of these things, he must apologize to the other child. The injured child determines whether the apology was sincere and appropriate for the injury. Sometimes, the offending child is asked to redo the apology to make it acceptable to the offended child. Apologies can be verbal or written. If a child hits another child, this is an automatic step four, which means an administrator calls the parent and the child is suspended from school for a day. The Responsive Classroom model creates a climate where the rules are clear to everybody.

As a result of this model, the climate and feeling of the school is calm, quiet, and orderly. This kind of feeling and atmosphere in the school creates a place where learning is enhanced and children feel secure. Teachers spend their time instructing their students rather than disciplining them. Children thrive when they know what is expected of them and where they can feel safe.

A major part of sustaining and maintaining relationships is the ability to regulate emotion. ADHD children mostly act out their feelings. This means that if an ADHD child is angry, he will very often insult, push, or even hit the child that made him angry. The ADHD child does not think about consequences. He simply acts on his feelings. He cannot and does not reflect on the best way to handle a painful situation. The ADHD child's impulsiveness does not allow for reflection. If he is hurt, he strikes. He cannot and does not take the time to reflect on the situation or his or the other person's feelings. He does not know how to regulate his emotions. If he feels restless, he will tap his feet, squirm, and move in his chair; or sometimes he will even walk around the room. If he knows the answer to a question, he will often call out the answer before the teacher asks him to respond. Raising his hand and waiting would require the ability to be patient and control his impulse. This inability to regulate emotion affects all aspects of his life, especially his relationships. Because the ADHD child acts on impulse, he often does not have any depth of emotion. Almost all hurtful situations are quickly forgotten. The ADHD child would more likely understand physical pain than emotional pain. This is because you can see physical pain. You know when you have a cut or broken a limb. Emotional pain is more subtle. You cannot see it. And often, it takes a fair amount of reflection to understand what just caused you pain. People who live in the now have a very hard time understanding and experiencing the subtleties and the depth of emotional pain. You cannot see it. You can only try to understand and experience emotional pain.

To have meaningful relationships, you have to recognize emotions in yourself and others. When another person is sad or hurt, it is important to be able to notice this feeling and respond appropriately. You would probably say to that person, "You seem sad today," "Can I help you?" or "Do you want to talk?"

In order to recognize sadness and feelings in others, you need to be able to step back and recognize how that other person is feeling. Because the ADHD child is mainly in the present, he cannot reflect on what another person is feeling. He is not able to take the time to analyze and think about the possibilities of how his friend might be feeling. Also, in order to recognize feelings in others, you need to be able to recognize feelings in yourself. You need to be able to label your own feelings accurately before you can label someone else's feelings. Identifying how somebody else feels is essential before you can understand and react appropriately to how they feel. All of these skills are very important in relationships. Identifying, regulating, and expressing feelings are all very difficult for the ADHD child. The reason for this is the ADHD child lives mostly in the present, and his actions, more often than not, are impulsive. As we have discussed, the capacity for reflecting, analyzing, understanding, and experiencing feelings depends on the ability to reflect and take the time necessary to be able to think and react appropriately to one's own and other people's emotions.

Probably the most difficult feeling to deal with is emotional hurt and pain. Almost everybody's immediate reaction to emotional hurt is anger. Emotional pain, in my opinion, most often is greater than physical pain. Recently, during a meeting with two children, one of the children made a comment that hurt the other child's feelings. This child we will call Rose. Rose immediately asked me for a sheet of paper and some crayons. She drew a picture of a heart and wrote "I love you" and gave it to the other girl we will call Patricia. Patricia stopped crying. Rose's gesture of kindness showed how sensitive she was to the other child. Rose immediately understood that Patricia was in pain. We cannot see emotional pain, nor can we use a Band-Aid or a pill to fix the problem. But emotional pain is real, and it is often hard to know what to do to alleviate the pain. Rose, being a very sensitive child, knew immediately what to do to alleviate Patricia's pain. I later asked Rose which is worse, physical pain or emotional pain. She is only seven years old yet she knew right away that emotional pain was worse than physical pain. The ADHD child has problems in handling emotional pain. Since he is often unable to understand his own feelings and pain, he does not know how to respond to other children's pain. Also, not having the capacity to let time heal, often his only answer is to strike out to get rid of the hurt.

Integration of appropriate social and emotional responses is hard for the ADHD child. The old adage that "one learns from one's mistakes" is very often not true of the ADHD child. Again, the inability of the ADHD child to self-reflect gets in the way of learning from his mistakes. Reflection, regulation of emotion, and integration of rules are all necessary skills to become socially and emotionally appropriate. If these skills are not learned, the possibility for personal growth is very limited.

I would like to share a story that exemplifies how the lack of integration in the ADHD child affects his social skills. Recently, I was talking to a teacher when a child asked her if he could go to the bathroom. The teacher says to the child, "How many times have I told you what to do when adults are talking? What are you supposed to say?" Child responds, "Excuse me." The teacher turns to me. She tells me "I must have told that child a hundred times to say excuse me." I responded that the child did not remember what to do because he is an ADHD child and that he does not have medication. The teacher says that she knows this about the child, but that she is going to tell him anyway. It would seem that this child did not integrate this social rule. Did this child not excuse himself because of a lack of intelligence? No. His ability to integrate social rules is greatly limited by his ADHD. He is too impulsive to think about the steps needed to get permission to go to the bathroom. Also there is little higher and sequential thinking in the ADHD child.

Chapter V

ADHD Behavior: What to Do

IT'S THE OTHER GUY

1. Hold your child accountable when he breaks the rules.

2. Teachers are usually fair.

3. Don't ask your child to tell you what happened.

4. Work with the administrator who has to discipline your child.

5. Give your child consequences for bad behavior

Most children with ADHD have problems with behavior in school and at home. This is a result of the hyperactivity, distractibility, focusing, and impulsiveness aspects of ADHD. Children with ADHD often are not hyper but have more difficulty with focusing, paying attention, and distractibility. Those children with the combined type of ADHD have problems in all of the above areas. Hyperactivity and impulse control are the two main factors why ADHD children have problems controlling their behavior. Most ADHD children do not think before they act. For example, if the teacher is doing a math lesson, the ADHD child could talk to another child, get out of his seat, and look out the window, or many other activities that distract him and the people around him. This is because Johnny does not think before he acts. The teacher could reprimand him one hundred times for the same problem, and still Johnny will do the same thing. Johnny never seems to learn from his mistakes. He keeps repeating the same mistakes over and over.

Parents are often surprised and skeptical that their child is having behavior problems in school. They will often tell me, the social worker, that their child is not a behavior problem at home. These parents are right. Their child is often not a behavior problem at home. Why is this? When an ADHD child is at home, the structure is more relaxed. He can play, watch TV, go outside, read a book, or whatever catches his or her fancy at the time. In school, however, the ADHD child has to sit still, has to focus, has to pay attention, and all the other behaviors that are needed for learning. Very often, parents don't truly become aware of their child's behavior problems until their child has to begin to do homework or other activities at home that require structure and discipline. Parents will say things like he is just a kid or he's young. In schools, however, as soon as a child enters kindergarten, even preschool, it becomes quickly evident that the child is ADHD. As I have already mentioned, being successful in school requires a child to function. At home, a child mostly plays and needs to function only when the parent asks him to do a task. School requires a child to function from the time he enters school until he leaves. Even recess is difficult for an ADHD child. Playing with other children means that the child needs to know and follow the rules of play like no hitting, no pushing, taking turns, etc. There are many reasons that parents have difficulty accepting that their child is having behavioral issues in school. The biggest reason is the one that we have explained: that school and home are very different environments with very different expectations. In school, a child needs to perform. At home, a child can play and the environment is less structured. Another reason parents have difficulty accepting that their child has a behavioral problem in school is that it is painful to hear that your child has a problem. I will explain this further in another chapter.

Over the centuries, society has developed rules of proper conduct. The Ten Commandments of the Bible tell us what is right and wrong. All religions tell us what they believe is proper behavior. In addition, all societies and nations develop their own rules of conduct. We could not have civilization without laws. Before any person can abide by the commandments or any rules of conduct whether they are religious or civil, that person needs to know, understand, accept, and internalize those rules of behavior. Children are not born knowing rules of behavior. It is something that they learn through their parents, through school, through religion and society. Of course, the first introduction to good behavior is the parents. Most children have a beginning idea of what good behavior means when they enter school and can behave accordingly. They are not perfect, as school is a new environment with different expectations than home. Teachers in kindergarten spend the first few weeks of school teaching the children the rules and expectations of their school. Much of what is taught in kindergarten is how to be good and how to get along with other children.

Learning and following rules of behavior continues throughout all our lives. That is because different parts of the country, different work environments, different religions, even different neighborhoods have their own special expectations and rules. Every day of our lives, we must make decisions about right and wrong. Making decisions about right and wrong becomes easier when these principles become part of our character. For the majority of people, making decisions about right and wrong becomes automatic most of the time. We don't even have to think about the right thing to do because the rules of behavior have become part of our fabric, our character, and our being. It is called conscience. Once you have developed a conscience, you have more time to pursue your passions, your work, and yourself and to take care of your family. People who do not have a conscience struggle with not getting into trouble and with being disciplined enough to pursue their dreams.

The ADHD child has many obstacles to understanding, internalizing, and following rules of behavior. Lack of focus, distractibility, impulsiveness, and hyperactivity all conspire against the ADHD child to develop a conscience and to make good decisions about proper behavior. If the teacher tells Sarah to sit down and pay attention, and Sarah continues to walk around the classroom and not pay attention, Sarah will not learn. Sitting quietly and paying attention are necessary for learning. Sarah, who is in second grade, may still learn, but not as much as she would if she were sitting still and paying attention. Sarah is not able to sit still because she has not internalized that this is a requirement of the classroom and for her to learn. There are two issues here: ability and conscience. Because Sarah cannot sit still and focus long enough to absorb what is being taught, she is not able to develop or internalize rules of behavior that would help her learn and behave appropriately. Even when Sarah sits quietly, her distractibility gets in her way. She misses a lot of what is being taught about all subjects and also about good behavior. Developing a conscience means learning and internalizing good rules of behavior. When ADHD is treated through medication and the symptoms of short attention span decrease, the child has a better chance of internalizing good rules of behavior and thinking before acting.

A child has to know what the rules are before he can follow them. Sitting quietly, focusing, and paying attention help a child to learn rules and develop a superego. Reducing impulsivity and hyperactivity helps a child follow these rules. Like most things in life, everything is relative. There is a range of severity when assessing ADHD in children. Some children are more impaired than others. This is contingent on many factors, such as the genes they were born with and the environment in which they live. Any child who is hyperactive, impulsive, and distractible cannot absorb a lot of knowledge being taught, which includes rules of behavior. The degree to which a child develops a conscience depends in large part to the degree and extent of their ADHD and how it is treated. Children who are diagnosed with ADHD without hyperactivity most often do not have a problem with behavior. They have difficulty with attention and distractibility, but not impulsiveness and hyperactivity.

As a parent, you can help your ADHD child by providing consistency and structure. Structure means making sure the schedule and routine are the same each day. This gives the ADHD child a better chance of doing what he has to do during the day. The day becomes routine for the child, and the child does not have to think about what to do next. Routine also makes for a peaceful and predictable household, which also benefits the ADHD child. Consistency means being predictable in all aspects of a child's life. Keeping the same schedule every day is just one aspect of being consistent. Parents need to be consistent in their rules, how they discipline, how they handle crises, and how they conduct themselves at all times. Parents are the main role models from whom children learn good behavior.

In school, teachers use many methods to teach children good behavior. As I mentioned, teachers spend at least the first two weeks of school to instruct children about what they expect from them. Every day, they begin by putting the day's schedule on the board where all children can see it. They often have ADHD children sit next to them and away from other children to minimize distractions and to provide structure for the ADHD child. This is very hard work and requires amazing patience. Very often, the social worker or psychologist in the school will help a teacher devise a behavior intervention plan. A BIP outlines for the child all of the behaviors he is having difficulty following during the day. They might include staying in his seat, raising his hand to ask a question, not talking to other children, looking at the teacher when she is talking, etc. A chart is kept each day to show the child and the teacher how well or how bad a child behaved during the day. If the child receives a certain number of points, he is usually given a reward at the end of the day. Also, the chart is often sent home every day, and the child may receive a reward at home for his good behavior. Rewards in school, depending on a child's age, could be a sticker, extra computer time, extra recess, or any other rewards that could work for that particular child. Rewards at home could include extra TV time, a later bedtime, a treat, time with a parent, or any other reward that works for that child. It should be noted that behavior plans are not a panacea. They do not work all the time and often help a child with some bad behaviors but not all. When a child is medicated, the results of a BIP are much improved. When a child cannot follow the rules of the school after all the above measures have been tried, he is sometimes given a personal assistant that stays with him all day. This assistant acts as the child's superego and helps him behave during the day.

In summary, good behavior is learned. It just does not happen by itself. Recently, a child I am seeing was getting into a lot of trouble because of his bad behavior. As a consequence, he did not get recess every time he did not follow the rules of the classroom. I asked him "What will happen if you continue to break the rules when you get older?" He answered that he would get bigger consequences. I replied, "Yes, like jail." I also praised him for his insight. His behavior has since improved greatly. Unlike many ADHD children, this child was able to reflect and change his behavior. The ADHD child is at a huge disadvantage to learn good behavior because of his distractibility, lack of focus, impulsiveness, and his hyperactivity. The ADHD child does not think before acting. As a result, he or she often does not develop a conscience, which could help him make good choices regarding right and wrong.

Chapter VI

Accepting That Your Child May Have ADHD

STOP THE MADNESS

1. Acceptance of possible ADHD is more helpful to your child than denial.

2. Learn to deal with the emotional pain of a diagnosis of ADHD.

3. Accept that ADHD is a medical problem.

4. Don't blame the teacher.

5. You and the school need to work together if your child has ADHD.

Although ADHD is an illness, it is different from other physical illnesses. If your child has a vision impairment, it can be easily remedied by wearing glasses. If your child is diabetic, it most likely can be handled by medication or by the use of insulin. A broken limb can be fixed by a cast. With ADHD, however, there is no obvious remedy. This is because ADHD has to do with a malfunction in the brain. The symptoms of ADHD are all abstract and cannot be seen. They include lack of attention, impulsivity, distractibility, and restlessness. It is most likely a left-brain problem.

As Jill Bolte Taylor informs us in her book, My Stroke of Insight, "To the right mind, no time exists other than the present moment and each moment is vibrant with sensation. Life or death occurs in the present moment. Our right hemisphere thinks in pictures and perceives the big picture of the present moment. Our left mind thrives on details, details, and more details about these details. Our left-hemisphere language centers use words to describe define, categorize, and communicate about everything. Our right mind evaluates the more subtle cues of language, including tone of voice, facial expression, and body language."[1]

What Dr. Taylor is telling us is that the two brain hemispheres work in tandem, but that through birth or brain injury or stroke, one or the other

---

[1]   *My Stroke of Insight* by Jill Bolte Taylor, PhD, pages 30 to 35

hemisphere is more dominant. The left hemisphere stresses details and is very important to executive functioning like working memory, internalization of self-directed speech, controlling emotions, motivation, and state of arousal and reconstitution. Working memory is the ability to hold information in your mind while working on a task. Internalization of speech is the ability to self-reflect and follow rules. Controlling emotions is the ability to think before reacting, like punching somebody if they made you angry. Reconstitution is the ability to break down observed behaviors in pursuit of a goal[2].

All adults and children have different degrees of ability in the areas mentioned above. Some of us are very good at working memory and focusing attention on a particular task. Others of us are disciplined and very goal oriented. Some of us are better than others at controlling our emotions. Still others are good at problem solving and following rules. The ADHD child is weak to varying degrees in all of the above areas. These weaknesses, by themselves, would not be a problem except when they begin to affect his functioning. The undiagnosed and untreated ADHD child often does not function to his ability because of the weaknesses mentioned above. This awareness and acceptance of a lack of functioning in your child is a key to diagnosing and getting help for your child. It is easy for parents to rationalize and say that every child has problems in one of the above areas. What parents need to acknowledge is that not every child has problems learning academics, social skills, and behavioral rules. Not every child is experiencing failure in one or the other of these areas. The ADHD child often does not make gains in one or more of these areas. For the ADHD child, these failures do not get better by themselves. The longer the ADHD child struggles without help, his problems progressively get worse. Not only does the ADHD child fail at learning, making friends, and following the rules, he often will develop poor self-esteem, lose his motivation to do well, get into trouble frequently, and become depressed, and sometimes even oppositional and defiant. Studies show that up to 60 percent of children with

---

[2]   Psychological Model of ADHD, Barkley

ADHD are at risk of developing oppositional defiant disorder[3]. There are many negative cumulative effects that develop when the ADHD child is not treated. We will discuss the treatment of ADHD in children in another chapter.

When the ADHD child is treated, success is possible. With help, the ADHD child can learn. He will begin to develop deep and lasting relationships with other children. He can begin to understand and regulate his own emotions. He will be able to empathize and connect with other children. He will begin to understand, retain, and follow the proper rules of behavior in school and at home. He will follow directions. He will understand consequences. ADHD children have difficulty in all of the above areas not because they want to misbehave and not learn but because they cannot pay attention. They cannot follow directions. They cannot sit still. They cannot follow rules. They cannot sustain long-term relationships. There is a huge difference between *cannot* and *won't*. All of the children I meet and counsel want to succeed and do well.

They are hampered in succeeding for many different reasons. Some are learning disabled. Some are ADHD. Others come from broken homes. Others have lost a parent or some other person in their lives. Others are depressed or have some other psychiatric illness. The common factor is that there are many different reasons why children struggle academically, behaviorally, and socially. Most times, parents are generally accepting of their child's lack of success in school if they can attribute it to a physical ailment, a death, a divorce, a move, or something concrete. The problem with ADHD, as we have explained, is that you cannot touch or feel it. It is something you are born with. If a parent has ADHD, there is at least a 57 percent chance or more that his or her child will have ADHD[4]. Oftentimes, the parent was never diagnosed as having ADHD. As a result, many parents are not even aware that they have ADHD. This makes it very difficult for them to accept that their child could have this illness. They believe that if they survived,

---

[3]   Sandra Reif, 1999

[4]   Shire US Inc.

their child will also survive. This is often true but not all the time. It does not have to be as hard for their child as it was for them. Also, parents with ADHD do not necessarily feel regret that they are ADHD. They are often very successful people. Many, many famous people probably had ADHD before anybody knew about this illness. Some examples are Thomas Edison, John Kennedy, Zsa Zsa Gabor, Jules Verne, John Lennon, and many others. The more successful a person is, the harder it would be for them to accept that their child has ADHD. In fact, the only reason to seek treatment for an ADHD child is he or she is not functioning in any of the areas in this book. These areas are *lack of functioning* with learning, with developing social relationships, and learning and following rules of behavior.

Unless they have serious problems, all parents want their children to succeed. Most parents would choose to go without something so that their child could get what they need and want. In poor countries, where there is sometimes not enough food, many parents will not eat so that their children will not go hungry. I think most parents have sacrificed something for their children, whether it be food, money, time, sleep, or something else. With ADHD, because the symptoms are abstract, it is harder for parents to accept that their children have problems. Also, the effects of ADHD seem like the kind of thing you could control. Most parents think that every child can be successful if only they work hard enough. Unfortunately, working and studying hard does not always result in success. The ADHD child, especially, because he cannot attend, focus, follow directions, and take the steps necessary to reach a goal, can work very hard, and still not succeed. Sometimes, the problems just mentioned are a result of other problems the child may have, like a divorce, a death of a parent, a move, or some other concrete situation. The kinds of problems are easier for children and parents to accept and address because they can be seen. This is not true with ADHD.

Another frequent explanation parents, teachers, and administrators give for the ADHD child's lack of success in school is that the child is behaving badly because he wants attention. I do not believe that ADHD and most other children behave badly to get attention. ADHD children do not wake up in the morning with the intent and desire to get in trouble in order to get attention. This would contradict the reality that most ADHD kids are impulsive. Impulsive means that they do not think before they act. They do not understand that when they behave badly, there are consequences. They can see that their behavior was bad only after it has happened. Consequences for not doing homework, for not listening to the teacher, or for fighting with other children are not usually pleasant or appealing. It is hard to imagine an ADHD child thinking, *I am not going to do my homework to make my parents angry*, or *I am going to punch my friend to get in trouble*. Impulsivity, the inability to think before acting, is the culprit here. It is what creates and causes the many bad choices ADHD children often make. All of what I am describing here seems obvious. If a child was blind, the parent would not expect his child to read. Yet if a child is impulsive, the parent expects his child to follow the rules at home and in school, to complete tasks on his own, to remember directions, and to have lasting friendships. It is natural and desirable for parents to have high expectations of their children. It is a major denial when the parents of an ADHD child expect him to get good grades, to follow rules, to have lots of friends, and to always succeed. All of the above expectations are impossible for the ADHD child to consistently accomplish without therapeutic help. Denial occurs as a defense against emotional and physical pain. As parents, we carry an added burden when we have children. Single people only have to deal with their own mistakes and failures. Parents also have to deal with the mistakes and failures of their children. This is very painful. Added to this pain is the enormous sense of helplessness when their child fails. With children, the level of sadness we feel is intensified because we not only identify with their pain, but we often feel helpless in trying to comfort them. We feel one with them and, at the same time, apart from them. Ultimately, we cannot control our children's behavior. This is not easy to accept. Many times, it is less painful to accept that our child has a problem than to deal with the pain and helplessness we feel. Of course, parents have the benefit of cheering and participating in their child's successes in school, sports, and other situations when they do well.

As we have explained, ADHD is a medical problem that impairs functioning. Still, parents have great difficulty accepting that their child has ADHD.

There are many reasons why parents cannot accept that their child may have ADHD. Because ADHD mainly affects behavior and lack of functioning, many parents of ADHD children feel they have failed as parents. This feeling of failure is very painful and therefore difficult to accept. It is even more painful if the parent was not diagnosed with ADHD and suffered through his childhood. No parent wants their child to experience the same hurt they felt as children. Parents will often say things like "He is just being a boy" or "He will grow out of it." Parents of ADHD children often cannot accept that their child cannot choose to do the right thing. It is too painful for the parent to accept that their child is failing in any way. People deal with pain in many different ways. To lessen the pain, parents will also blame themselves. They will think that they have not set good rules. Self-blame is how some parents handle their children's struggles and failures.

Other parents blame the teacher if their child is not doing well in school. They will tell the teacher that their child is good at home. These parents do not understand that school is very different from home. The ADHD child can often meet the demands of home, but not of school. They will challenge the teacher. They will say to the teacher or me, "You are not a doctor. How do you know that my child has ADHD?" If a child is not learning, they will say that their child has a learning disability rather than accept that their child can't pay attention. If their child does not behave, they will say that the teacher is too demanding. If their child gets in trouble with another child, they will blame the other child. Other parents will attribute their child's hyperactivity and impulsiveness to their child's diet. Studies have shown that diet, especially sugar, has nothing to do with ADHD. Parents have many explanations for their child's lack of functioning. The reason for this is that to accept that your child has a disability is to accept the emotional pain. Pain and loss is very hard to experience. Emotional pain does not just go away and disappear. It has to be worked through. As parents know, the pain they feel when their child is ill, suffering, or dies is worse than any pain they could experience. This is because not only you feel your child's pain but also you feel helpless to do anything about it. A sister-in-law of mine who lost her daughter over twenty-five years ago says that she thinks of her every day. Even when her mother and sister died, she did not feel as bad as when her daughter died. This mother will never forget her daughter. The death of a child is the worst experience a parent could have. There are many other losses parents experience with their children. Their children's success is also their success. Their children's failure is their failure as well. When the teacher tells a parent that their child is not doing well in school, the parent often experiences this information as personal criticism or failure. Children are part of us. If they hurt, we hurt. Their joy is our joy. For many parents, telling them that their child is not doing well in school is worse than somebody saying that they did not do well on their job. We want to help, but often, we do not know what to do. We feel one with our children, and at the same time, we feel apart from them. Ultimately, we cannot control our children's behavior, successes, or losses. This realization does not make our pain any easier.

Chapter VII

What to Do About Treatment

TIME TO GET REAL

1. Seek medical treatment.

2. Give your child medication if your doctor recommends it.

3. Let the teacher know that you have given your child medication.

4. Don't blame the school if your child fails and develops low self-esteem.

5. Without help for ADHD, your child could become oppositional and defiant.

Recent studies show that about 8 percent of the population of children up to eighteen years old has a form of ADHD. This means that in a classroom of twenty-five children, there is at least one child with ADHD. The majority of children with ADHD are boys. Girls also have ADHD, but usually of the inattentive type. According to longtitudinal studies done by Timothy Wilens, M.D. at the Harvard Medical School, the persistence of ADHD from latency-aged children into adolescence is 70 percent. About 30 to 40 percent of grown-up ADHD children generally do well. Furthermore, 30 to 50 percent have symptoms into adulthood; 10 to 20 percent of adults with ADHD have significant impairment and disability. It is important to note that these statistics mostly have to do with children who are not treated for ADHD.

The above statistics means that millions of children have ADHD. Unfortunately, many children are not treated for ADHD. The consequences of not treating ADHD are very severe. Not treating ADHD affects all aspects of a child's life, including intellectual, social, emotional, and moral development. Over the last several years, there has been a movement among many parents to not allow teachers to talk about ADHD and medication. In Connecticut, teachers who speak about ADHD and medication are considered breaking the law and could face penalties. Fortunately, the law allows school social workers and nurses to talk about ADHD with parents. In many schools in Connecticut, elaborate procedures have been established to determine if a child has ADHD. This includes the completion of a Connors' Rating Scale by the teacher and the parent. According to federal law, ADHD is seen as a medical issue, not an educational one. This means that a child with a diagnosis of ADHD would need to be labeled as health impaired in order to receive special education services. A diagnosis from a physician, school psychologist, or social worker would be necessary to get a diagnosis of ADHD. Unfortunately, many parents do not accept the diagnosis of ADHD. This rejection that ADHD is a medical problem has very negative consequences for their child.

My experience is that a majority of parents and some teachers reject the reality that ADHD is a medical problem. The reason for this rejection has less to do with it being a medical diagnosis and mostly has something to do with medication being the recommended treatment. This bias against medication comes from many sources, but mostly from reports by the press that medication for ADHD does not work and is harmful. The press often does not even take the time to study and report on the millions of instances where medication was helpful and changed children's lives for the better. Recently, in a new book published this year, the author, Judith Warner started out writing a book about how children are medicated too much. After six years of research and talking to parents, she concluded that children are not medicated enough.

The fact is that the use of medication for the treatment of ADHD has been around since the early seventies and has been helpful to millions of children. Many studies have been done about the benefits of medication therapy for ADHD in children. One of the best and most long-term studies was done by the National Institute of Mental Health over the past ten years. At fourteen and twenty-four months, the best results occurred in children who received medication alone or in combination with psychosocial therapy. In a surprise, the relative advantage of drug therapy began to fade at the twenty-fourth month and completely disappeared at the thirty-six-month mark. The side effects of these medications are most often mild and transient. The most common side effects are loss of appetite, weight loss, insomnia, and headaches[5].

---

[5]   Harvard Mental Health Letter, October 2008

Some parents are fearful that medicating their child for ADHD could cause medical problems like high blood pressure and heart rate irregularities. Studies have shown that ADHD drugs are not likely to cause cardiac risk in anyone who does not already have a risk for heart problems. Clearly, a thorough medical history needs to be taken by the pediatrician or a child psychiatrist before any type of medication is administered to a child. Also, some parents and doctors have been concerned that ADHD drugs could cause growth suppression. One study of seven to nine-year-olds showed that those who had continuously taken drugs for two years were, on average, half an inch shorter and eight pounds lighter than those not taking the medication. Teachers and parents are also worried that using drugs when their children are little might mean that their children might abuse drugs when they get older. These fears are not true. A recent *Harvard Mental Health Letter* in June of 2008 indicates that there is no link between use of stimulants in children and later use of alcohol, tobacco, or drugs of any kind[6].

I would say that there is a *greater* likelihood that children who are not treated for ADHD will eventually use drugs, alcohol, or tobacco as adolescents and adults. Studies show that adolescents who have nonrelated ADHD have a 64 percent chance of being dependent on drugs or tobacco and a 33 percent chance of abusing drugs[7].

As has been mentioned, medication for ADHD has been available for over thirty years. Initially, the main medication was Ritalin. Ritalin, like many of the other medications that have come out over time, is a stimulant. Reaction to Ritalin and other stimulants is very fast. It takes about an hour for the drug to take effect and lasts for about three to four hours. Now, Ritalin and many other stimulants that are long acting have been developed. One of the more popular of these is Adderall XR. The benefit of this medication is that it will last up to twelve hours. This is very good and effective in that the medication can be taken

---

[6]   Harvard Letter, June 2008

[7]   Wilens, "Impact of ADHD and Its Treatment on Substance Abuse," Harvard Medical School [April 2006]

in the morning and last all day, especially during the important homework time. Side effects are mild for the most part. Also, one of the benefits of stimulants is that they work right away. Unlike other medications, stimulants last only for the time intended: three hours for ordinary Adderall, and about twelve hours for the long-acting type. Stimulant medications are the most widely prescribed class of medications. The other type of medications used for ADHD is not stimulants. These medications are more recent. The most common of these medications is Strattera, which is a selective norepinephrine reuptake inhibitor. Another name for this type of medication is atomoxetine. Of the two types, in a recent study, the use of long-acting stimulant medication provided a more consistent and reliable pattern of symptom improvement than atomoxetine. Symptom improvement was seen in subjective measures of behavior, attention, academic productivity, and an overall measure of global improvement. Another advantage to stimulant medication is that parents can choose not to give the medication on weekends and during summer vacation. Strattera takes a longer period to develop in the system to work. This means that parents cannot skip doses, even on the weekends[8].

The most important aspect of medication for ADHD is that it is essential for the ADHD child to *function*. Social, behavioral, family, and individual therapy are adjuncts to medication. Since ADHD is a brain dysfunction, medication is essential to give the *ADHD brain time to process information, regulate emotion, attend to information, and make good choices.* For these reasons, the ADHD child needs medication to be able to learn, to make friends, and to follow the rules. Medication gives the ADHD child the tools needed for learning like being focused and paying attention. Medication reduces impulsivity and allows the ADHD child to think before acting. When a child functions well in school, his self-esteem increases. The child is happy, and parents are also pleased. If this is true, how is it that many parents do not accept that their child has ADHD, much less accept that medication is necessary for treatment? There are many reasons why parents do not and cannot accept the reality of ADHD and the

---

[8]   Journal of Attention Disorders, August 2005

detrimental consequences of not seeking help for their ADHD child. Most of these reasons have to do with fear, anxiety, and loss.

As we discussed in a previous chapter, accepting that your child has ADHD is not easy. All parents want their children to be perfect. Children are an extension of themselves. If their child is not perfect, then they are not perfect. There is a real, painful, intense, and genuine sense of loss that occurs when a parent hears that their child is not doing well in school. When the teacher reports that their child is not learning because he cannot attend, focus, or is distractible, the parent feels hurt, loss, anger, and many other feelings. Some parents get angry. They feel that the teacher is not doing enough to help their child. Other parents feel that the teacher is telling them that they are not doing a good job. Still, others think that their child has allergies, a thyroid dysfunction, or some other physical problem to explain why their child is not doing well in school. One thing for sure is that all of these reactions are a result of emotional pain and loss. Parents hurt deeply when they hear something negative about their child. That feeling is real. Emotional pain is often far worse than physical pain. With the right help, physical pain can be reduced or go away. Emotional hurt and loss requires a working through of the emotional pain. This is hard work. Denial and projection are frequent ways people use to deal with emotional pain. The problem is that denial and projection don't help resolve the problem. Denial is when the person minimizes the problem so as not to experience emotional pain. Projection is when the person blames somebody else for the problem. To help your child who has ADHD and that medication is necessary for the treatment of ADHD, you (the parent) need to reach a point of intellectual and emotional acceptance. In the previous chapter, we discussed the many reasons why intellectually it makes sense to accept a diagnosis of ADHD. In this chapter, we would like you to accept intellectually and emotionally that the principal treatment for ADHD needs to start with medication.

Many parents do not accept medication as an option because of the difficulty every parent has in accepting that their child has limitations. Children are often felt by parents to be an extension of themselves. There is a real, intense, and genuine sense of loss that occurs when a parent hears from the teacher for the first time that their child is not learning because he cannot pay attention, focus, and is distracted. This kind of criticism is intangible, not concrete. Often, parents interpret not paying attention as a lack of motivation. Like most children, ADHD children want to please their parents by succeeding in school. The problem is they can't. Try as they may, they can't pay attention long enough to retain and understand what is being taught in class. They also have too many distractions. They want to focus but cannot. Many of these children simply stop trying after a while. They begin to feel that they are stupid. Self-esteem plummets. They stop caring about school.

Denial is very strong in all of us. None of us want to accept our limitations and failures. We have an even more difficult time accepting the limitations and failures of our children. As parents, we want to protect our children from all harm. When teachers and other professionals tell us that our child is struggling in school, it sometimes feels like they are criticizing not only our child but also us as parents.

Ninety-five percent of parents I meet are doing their best to meet the physical, social, emotional, and intellectual needs of their children. It is hard for these parents to accept that even while they are doing their best, their children are still having problems. To believe and trust what teachers are saying about your child, especially if it's negative, means listening to somebody else's advice about what is best for your child. This is not easy for a parent to do. It means giving up control. It means trusting somebody else's opinion about what is best for your child. As adults, we sometimes have difficulty putting trust in our doctors regarding our own well-being. For many parents, it is even harder to put trust in doctors and other professionals with regard to their child's health. This is one of the reasons parents are often reluctant to give their child medication even though it would be helpful.

Of course, medication is not the only form of treatment for ADHD, but research has shown that it is the most effective. Individual and group therapy, as well as family therapy, have also proved to be helpful. Of the different types of therapies, though, medication shows the best results. Recent research also shows that medication therapy begins to fade after the twenty-four-month mark and completely disappears by the thirty-sixth month in children who consistently took the medication. This could mean that children who were transitioned back into community-based care were not monitored as closely as they had been in the study. It could also mean that medication helped the brain correct itself. The left side of the brain was able to absorb and retain the skills needed to learn, to socialize, and to behave. These skills, once learned, appear to continue even after medication is stopped. It would seem that during the medication period, impulsivity lessened, organizational skills, attention, and focus increased, and the child learned to make better choices. Of course, these conclusions would need to be validated by long-term research. I do believe that prompt and early treatment of ADHD reduces the risk of a child developing further problems like opposition defiant disorder and other comorbid diagnoses.

Emotional acceptance is more difficult than intellectual acceptance. Emotional acceptance means experiencing and going through a grieving process. Acknowledging that your child has ADHD is a major loss. The first reaction is most often denial that a problem exists and that does it have to be somebody else's problem. When it becomes clear over time that the problem is not going away with your help, the teacher's help, or the therapist's help, then reality sets in and you (the parent) often become angry. You probably also begin to feel inadequate or guilty that your child has ADHD. Next, you begin to feel sad that you, your child, and your family have this problem. Last, but most important, you reach a point of acceptance where you begin to see the problem for what it is—a malfunction of the brain—and begin to seek help. At this point, also accepting that medication is needed to help your child becomes possible. After your child has begun to take medication and you see that it is helping him or her function in school and at home, you can breathe a huge sigh of relief. You are happier. Your child is happier, and more importantly, he can begin to function in school behaviorally, socially, and academically. Your child's self-esteem will increase. Best of all, your child will have a better chance to develop into a functioning, productive, and happy adult.

Chapter VIII

Consequences of Not Treating ADHD

THE SLIPPERY SLOPE

1. Not treating ADHD can often lead to more problems for your child.

2. Yes. Learning, social, and behavioral problems can get worse.

3. Your child could become insecure and obsessive.

4. Your child could become anxious and depressed.

5. Your child could become oppositional, defiant, and eventually develop a conduct disorder.

When ADHD is not treated, the symptoms often get worse, and children develop other problems like oppositional defiant disorder, conduct disorder, depression, and anxiety. Although ADHD is a physical and neurological disorder, it is not the physical manifestations that become worse like untreated diabetes, heart disease, or cancer. As we have learned, the consequences of not treating ADHD manifest themselves in three important aspects of a child's life: learning, social-emotional development, and behavior.

When a child enters kindergarten, social and behavioral development is emphasized. This is the child's introduction to school. Still, there is some learning that takes place like learning the alphabet, numbers, and colors. Starting in first grade, the emphasis in school increasingly becomes about developing skills and academic learning.

Very often, the ADHD child does well in kindergarten and the first grade. However, by second grade, his struggles begin with academics, and there is an increase in social and behavioral demands. The child wants to learn, but his short attention span, distractibility, lack of focus, and lack of impulse control make school increasingly challenging. The child begins to lose interest in school, starts not following the rules, and does not get along with the teacher and other children. This trend continues into third grade, where many children with ADHD hit the wall. In most schools, the academic expectations and curriculum in third grade are a major jump from second grade. Many children with untreated ADHD are unable to meet the demands of third grade. This is because they often missed out on learning important concepts that they need to build on in third grade. As a result, they lose confidence, start acting out, and very often develop low self-esteem and begin to not care about school. School becomes like being in a prison cell with no possibility of escape. Every day, the children fail at something, whether it is learning, behavior, or making and keeping friends. They begin to not care.

Instead of trying to behave, they ignore the rules, don't listen to the teacher, and become discipline problems. This begins a vicious cycle. The more they get in trouble and fail, the more they stop caring about learning and the consequences of their behavior. They become oppositional and defiant. For many, being suspended becomes a good experience. It is better for them to be suspended and be at home than to have to endure another day of school. This becomes a sad state of affairs for everybody involved, including the child, the teacher, and the parent.

Failure breeds more failure. All of the children I have worked with over the years want to succeed; that is, until school becomes so frustrating that they stop caring. As a child with untreated ADHD moves into the fourth and fifth grades, the educational, social, and behavioral demands become more difficult to meet. School becomes an experience of failure, not success.

Most children with ADHD are capable and intelligent people. The ability is there but not the skills needed to succeed and learn. Learning requires attention, organization, focus, memory, and the ability to follow directions. By fifth grade in our school, children are expected to complete projects on their own and to meet the deadlines established by the teacher. This means that they need to establish a schedule and have the ability to understand the requirements of the project, the steps they need to take to complete the project and to establish a timeline for when it needs to be done. By fifth grade, most children are able to finish projects on their own. The untreated ADHD child very often does not have the skills needed to do independent work. Working independently is essential to learning as a child moves into junior high school and college. In short, the ADHD child often has the ability but not the skills needed to succeed in school. In our school, we have an after-school program called the Homework Club that teaches students the skills they need to succeed in school.

Like all the other children in school, by the time the ADHD child reaches fifth grade, he is expected to behave independently and to be an example for the younger children in the school. The untreated ADHD child very often does not have the skills needed to behave independently. He often still needs reminders to do what is expected of him. The ADHD child, as we know, does not think before he acts. He acts impulsively. To behave well, a child has to have internalized the rules he needs to follow in school. He also needs to have the discipline to follow the rules.

Socially, children in fifth grade have learned how to make friends and get along with people. There still may be some teasing, fighting, and provoking, but they mostly are under control. By fifth grade, when teased or provoked, most children have learned to ignore these taunts. They do not, for the most part, react by hitting and fighting when angry. They have learned to talk about their feelings rather than act them out. They have learned how to engage people in conversation. The untreated ADHD child very often has not learned these skills by fifth grade. He is still taunting, teasing, arguing, breaking the rules, and sometimes even hitting other children when angry.

When reprimanded for not being responsible for his learning, for not following the rules, or for not getting along with others, the untreated child sometimes becomes oppositional and defiant. "This condition is characterized by the child often losing his temper, arguing with adults, deliberately doing things that will annoy other people, not complying with the requests or rules of adults, blaming others for their mistakes, being easily annoyed by others, being spiteful or vindictive, or being angry or resentful."

This condition is listed in the *Diagnostic and Statistical Manual of Mental Disorders*, the *DSM-IV Revised*. ADHD is common in children with children with oppositional defiant disorder[9]. There is evidence that ADHD, if left untreated, results in a greater possibility of ODD. According to the *DSM-IV-TR*, "Approximately half of clinic-children with Attention-Deficit Hyperactivity Disorder have Oppositional Defiant Disorder or Conduct Disorder"[10].

Conduct disorder can be diagnosed only in children who have turned eighteen. Some children who develop conduct disorder were also diagnosed as oppositional defiant disorder when they were younger. Children with this disorder "may display threatening or intimidating behavior, initiate frequent physical fights, use a weapon, be physically cruel to people, steal while confronting a victim, or force someone into sexual activity"[11]. Again, about half of people referred to a clinic for conduct disorder also have ADHD, the individual or combined type.

As we can see, the consequences of not treating ADHD are many and severe. When children are not treated for ADHD, they often hit the wall, are unable to function in school, get along with peers, and behave appropriately. About half of them develop ODD or CD. Also, untreated ADHD often leads to substance abuse problems. Many of these children later also end up in prison. Children who have ADD, that is, without the hyperactivity, are also affected by their condition. They have trouble learning because they are easily distracted, cannot focus and pay attention. Many become depressed or anxious and have low self-esteem. One child I saw with ADD was very motivated to learn. He was very creative and could remember in great detail subjects that interested him. For example, he could tell me everything about airplanes, like the number of passengers the plane could carry, the model, and when it was

---

[9]   DSMR-IV, p 100

[10]   p. 88

[11]   DSM-IV-TR, p. 94

built. He would create three-dimensional models of airplanes with exquisite detail from paper. In school, however, he was often frustrated and anxious. He wanted everything he did to be perfect. If he got one wrong answer on a test, he felt as if he failed. His self-esteem was very low. It took a while, but he and I were eventually able to help him find ways to not expect so much of himself. As he became more accepting of his mistakes, he began to do better in school, and his self-esteem improved dramatically. This boy had a mild case of ADD. He just needed some strategies to feel better about himself when he did not know the answer or made mistakes on tests.

As children grow into adolescence and adulthood, the untreated ADHD child often experiences failure after failure. Many times, the ADHD adolescent and adult end up without work and even in prison. Estimates of the number of people in prison with ADHD ranges from 9 percent to 45 percent. Many ADHD adults are successful. However, the road to adulthood often was filled with much frustration, hardship, and failure. Many ADHD adults I have treated describe childhoods filled with frustration and failure, especially in school. Many arrive at their career of choice late in life, having been delayed by many false starts and having to make up for past mistakes.

Chapter IX

Please Understand Me, I am Your Child

1. If you accept me as I am, I will have a better chance at success.

2. You will be better parents and I will have an edge.

3. I will learn more and get good grades.

4. I will have good and lasting relationships.

5. I will be happy, confident, well behaved, and successful.

"I am your child. I want to learn. I want to control my feelings, especially my anger. I want to make and keep friends. I do not want to be bad. I want to listen to my teacher. I want to feel good about myself. Mostly, I want to make you, my parents, happy and proud of me."

Children are happiest when they are successful, motivated, and learning. ADHD children, if they are not treated, often become frustrated, lose their self-esteem, and stop caring. Some even become oppositional and defiant. Many try their best but *cannot* meet the demands of their teachers and parents. Some children, especially those who want to do everything well, sometimes become anxious and feel like they are failures in school. Many other children simply stop caring about doing well. They give up trying. This is a real loss to everybody—parents, teachers, but mostly to themselves. My saddest moments with children are when I see that they have stopped caring. Most of them have tried to be successful but cannot meet the demands placed on them. Rather than continue to become frustrated, they surrender and stop caring about school. Who can blame them? As I have said earlier, there is a major difference between can't and won't. Even if ADHD children *want* to do what is asked of them, they often *cannot* do it. After a while, when a person cannot do something, he or she usually gives up.

"I am not bad. When I threw the eraser at my friend, I was just being funny. When I threw my pen at the ceiling while the teacher was giving a lesson, I was bored. The teacher was angry because I pushed another child. I did not mean to do it. I'm not bad."

"I am always in trouble. When my parents told me to brush my teeth, take a shower, and go to bed, they got mad at me. I just forgot to do everything. Oh yeah, and I forgot to do my project for school. The teacher was angry. I just forgot."

When a parent says, "My child does not want to listen to me," that parent does not understand the difference between can't and won't in their ADHD child. The ADHD child does not follow directions because he can't remember all of the directions or gets distracted while he is trying to do them. The ADHD child is not being bad when he is not sitting still in class; he can't sit still. He is not being bad when he is not focused in class; he can't focus because he cannot pay sustained attention and is easily distracted. The ADHD child does not follow the rules in class because he has not internalized them. Parents need to understand and accept their child's limitations. Unfortunately, all of the characteristics of ADHD children described in this book limit their success in school. This is not because the ADHD child is not smart or capable. He often is at least average to above average in intelligence. He is not successful because he lacks the tools necessary to do well in school like being able to focus, pay attention, and sit still. Also, his brain's executive functions like memory, planning, organizing, and decision making are weak. These attributes are essential to a child's success in school. Without them, it is very difficult to learn all that is needed to move from grade to grade. As we have discussed, school becomes harder, not easier. We can help our ADHD child by accepting him as he is. He is not bad. He is impaired. He has a medical problem that is neurologically based.

Many parents doubt that their child has ADHD because he does not have any problems at home. ADHD children often do not have many problems at home, except for homework, following directions, and not interrupting adults.

This is because home is not structured like school. The ADHD child can do things at home when he wants, not when the teacher tells him. At home, there is less structure and there are less demands. Home is a much different place than school. Also, at home, the ADHD child has computer games, TV, and many other distractions. School is structured and very demanding. Also, it is a long day. If you look back on your childhood, I am sure that you would remember as I do that a day in school seemed like an eternity. When an ADHD child returns home after school, he is often relieved and happy to be home where he is free to do what he wants. The main problems for him would be doing homework and following directions.

"I must be stupid. I can't learn. I give up. School is too hard. I always have to sit next to the teacher. I forgot what she told me. I left my social studies book at home, again. I hope the teacher will not ask me a question. I was looking out the window and did not hear what she said. I hate doing homework and special projects."

Your ADHD child is intelligent. Why can't he learn and do well in school?

His difficulty with learning has something to do with his brain. His brain often does not allow him to have sustained attention, good memory, and organizational skills to sit still and to be able to follow directions. These skills, as you know, are essential to learning. Since schools build from grade to grade on what has been previously taught, many ADHD children fall further behind academically from year to year. This is because they often miss important information from year to year that they need for the next year of instruction.

"I just want to have fun. I like to play. When I said Joe was stupid, I was just joking. I don't know why he is mad. The teacher said I should apologize. I did."

"'Ha-ha! I was only joking Joe.' The teacher and Joe did not think I meant it. They said I should apologize again. I got mad and walked away."

ADHD children often have a lot of friends. This is because they have a lot of energy and are fun to be with. The problem is that these friends often do not last. The ADHD child is for the moment. His relationships tend to be superficial. He can be angry one minute and happy the next. ADHD children lack impulse control and empathy. These are the two main reasons ADHD children have difficulty with closeness, intimacy, and making lasting friends.

Parents can help by being consistent in their expectations of their children. They should have clear and consistent expectations of their children. For example, hitting somebody because you are angry is always wrong, not just sometimes. They should not blame the victim or minimize the severity of their children's problems with other children. This is not easy to do because it is easier to blame than to accept the pain that your child did something wrong and disappointed you.

In this book, I have tried to help parents understand, accept, and help their children.

The majority of parents love their children and want them to succeed. The truth is that ADHD children are easy to love. They respond immediately and positively to the fun things you do with them like playing a game, taking a trip, watching a movie, taking a walk, and many other activities. The problem is that ADHD children can also be very frustrating and difficult to parent. Doing homework, chores, getting ready for school, going to bed, remembering all they need for school require parents' constant involvement. This is tiring, demanding, and frustrating for many parents. Even with parents' best efforts, their children still have problems, especially in school. Since school is where most of their children's problems manifest themselves, many parents conclude that the schools are not doing enough for their children. This is not true. Most schools do everything they can to help children learn. No school wants to have the reputation of being a school where children do not learn. The fact is, as we have explained in this book, that ADHD children face many obstacles to learning, social interaction, and following school rules. The characteristics that impede a child's learning are distractibility, impulsiveness, short attention span, and lack of executive functioning. As we have learned, these characteristic have to do with the way the brain functions in ADHD children.

No parent wants to think that their child's problems are a result of genetics. Many parents deny the severity of their children's problems. Many other parents project blame on teachers and the school when their children do not succeed. They blame other kids or the school when their children get in trouble. It is hard for parents to accept that their child may have ADHD. Acceptance of a child's difficulties is emotionally painful. Denial and blame are much less painful. But they are not helpful to your child. The best help you can give your ADHD child is accept that he has that condition and seek medical help. Medical help will allow your child to focus, pay attention, and be less impulsive. Medical help should be accompanied by therapy with a skilled professional like a social worker. This therapy will help your child internalize the social, educational, and behavioral skills that your child needs to be successful. If your child had diabetes, a heart problem, bad eyesight, or a loss of hearing, you would take him to the doctor. If ADHD is a medical diagnosis, then seeing a doctor only makes sense. Yet many parents still do not want to take this step. I believe they do not take this step because they think that their child is being willful when he is not paying attention, not behaving, not doing his homework, and not following the rules. As I have explained, there is a huge difference between can't and won't. Also I think that parents do not take their children to the doctor because they do not want to give their children medication. This is most often the recommended medical treatment for ADHD.

Schools and parents should provide the ADHD child with the tools needed to succeed academically, socially, and behaviorally. As Hillary Clinton says, "It takes a village." Children succeed the most when all the people involved with them work together as a team. This includes principals, teachers, social workers, school psychologists, parents, doctors, and all adults who interact with them.

About The Author

Henry Mainville, M.S.W. is a psychotherapist with over thirty years of experience treating children and families in a variety of settings. For the past twenty years, he has been working with children and families in the public school system. He also has a private practice in Stamford, CT. treating families,couples, children and individuals. If you would like to know more about Henry Mainville and how to reach him, please check his website.

CONCLUSION

<u>PLEASE UNDERSTAND ME, I AM YOUR CHILD</u>

BIBLIOGRAPHY

DSMR-IV-TR
2000

Harvard Mental Health Letter
Harvard Medical School
2005-2010

Journal of Attention Disorders
August 2005

My Stroke of Insight
Jill Bolt Taylor, Ph.D.

Psychological Model of ADHD
Barkely, Shire Pharmaceuticals

Publications
Shire Pharmaceuticals, U.S.A.

We've Got Issues
Judith Warner